Berger Science Readers

SNAP!

A Book About
Alligators and
Crocodiles

For Hana, with much love
—M.B. and G.B.

Special thanks to Paul L. Sieswerda
of the New York Aquarium
for his expertise

Photography credits:
Cover: Tom McHugh/Photo Researchers, Inc.; Back Cover: Wolfgang Bayer/Bruce Coleman Inc.; page 1: Frank Krahmer/Bruce Coleman Inc.; page 3: Tom McHugh/Photo Researchers, Inc.; pages 4-5: E. R. Degginger/Photo Researchers, Inc.; page 6: Jack Couffer/Bruce Coleman Inc.; page 7: Stephen J. Krasemann/Photo Researchers, Inc.; page 8: Alan D. Carey/Photo Researchers, Inc.; page 9: Tom & Pat Leeson/Photo Researchers, Inc.; page 11: David Austen/Stone/Getty Images; page 12: Robert Hermes/Photo Researchers, Inc.; page 13: Wendell Metzen/Bruce Coleman Inc.; page 14: Treat Davidson/Photo Researchers, Inc.; page 15: CC Lockwood/Photo Researchers, Inc.; page 16: Wolfgang Bayer/Bruce Coleman Inc.; page 17: Dr. Robert Potts Jr./Photo Researchers, Inc.; page 18: Nigel J. Dennis/Photo Researchers, Inc.; page 19 (top): Roy Morsch/Bruce Coleman Inc.; page 19 (bottom): Harold Hoffman/Photo Researchers, Inc.; page 20 (top): Dr. Robert Potts Jr./Photo Researchers, Inc.; page 20 (bottom): David T. Roberts/Nature's Images, Inc./Photo Researchers, Inc.; page 21: Bill Goulet/Bruce Coleman Inc.; pages 22-23: John Serrao/Photo Researchers, Inc.; page 24: James Prince/Photo Researchers, Inc.; page 25: Gary Retherford/Photo Researchers, Inc.; page 27 (all): Charles V. Angelo/Photo Researchers, Inc.; page 28: Byron Jorjorian/Bruce Coleman Inc.; page 29: Stephen Cooper/Stone/Getty Images; page 30: Root/Okapia/PR/ Photo Researchers, Inc.; page 32: Wolfgang Bayer/Bruce Coleman Inc.; page 33: The Purcell Team/CORBIS; pages 34-35: Larry Allan/Bruce Coleman Inc.; page 36: Frank Krahmer/Bruce Coleman Inc.; page 37: Gary Retherford/Photo Researchers, Inc.; page 38: Jeff Foott/Bruce Coleman Inc.; page 39 (top): Bill Bachman/Photo Researchers, Inc.; page 39 (bottom): Mary Beth Angelo/Photo Researchers, Inc.; Photo Research: Sarah Longacre

ISBN 0-439-80181-8

12 11 10 9 8 7 6 5 4 3 2 1   6 7 8 9 10 11/0

Printed in the U.S.A.
First revised edition, April 2006

Berger Science Readers

SNAP!

A Book About Alligators and Crocodiles

by Melvin & Gilda Berger

SCHOLASTIC INC.
New York Toronto London Auckland Sydney
Mexico City New Delhi Hong Kong Buenos Aires

Chapter One

Lumpy and Bumpy

A giant alligator floats in the water. You can hardly see its body. Most of it is hidden. You might think it's a lumpy, bumpy log.

Look carefully. Can you spot the alligator's eyes? They stick up above the water. They let the alligator see all around.

The alligator's nostrils also stick up above the water. That's a very good thing. The alligator can breathe and hide under the water at the same time!

The alligator lies still. It waits and watches. In a while, a very large fish swims by.

Suddenly the alligator flings open its huge jaws. *SNAP!* It catches the fish with its many sharp teeth. The fish tries to break free. But the alligator holds on tightly.

Soon the fish stops wriggling. The alligator juggles the fish around in its jaws. It gets the fish into the right place for swallowing. The alligator jerks back its head. And the fish slides down its throat!

The alligator swims to the riverbank. It slowly climbs out of the water. It walks on its four short legs. Its long tail drags behind.

Suppose you happened to walk by. You might think the alligator was a crocodile. The two animals look very much alike.

How can you tell an alligator from a crocodile?

Chapter Two

Alike, but Different

The alligator has a long, lumpy, bumpy body. So does the crocodile. The alligator has four short legs, sharp teeth, and a long, strong tail. So does the crocodile.

But alligators and crocodiles are not exact look-alikes. They have different noses, or snouts.

An alligator has a wide, rounded snout. It looks like the letter U. A crocodile's snout comes to a point. It looks more like the letter V.

There is another important difference. You can see it when the animals' mouths are closed. Alligators just show their top teeth. Crocodiles show both top and bottom teeth.

Crocodiles are usually longer than alligators. They can also outswim alligators. Most crocodiles weigh more, too. That may be why crocodiles are better fighters.

Alligators and crocodiles often wait quietly for their dinner. They lie hidden in the water. They wait for fish and other animals they want to eat.

Both alligators and crocodiles live in lakes, swamps, and rivers. But alligators live only in the southern United States and in China. You can find crocodiles all over the world.

Chapter Three

Mothers and Babies

In spring, the alligators and crocodiles are busy. They start to build their nests. The nests are on land. But they are always near water.

The female alligator shovels with her hind legs. She scoops grass, twigs, and leaves into a big heap.

Soon she has a huge nest. It may be as big as a king-sized bed. And it may be as tall as a first grader. The alligator then crawls all over the nest. She packs it down with her heavy body.

The female crocodile usually makes a more simple nest. She just digs a hole in the sand. Or she makes a pile of twigs, grass, and mud.

The female alligator or crocodile lays from 20 to 60 eggs in her nest. The eggs are white. They look like the chicken eggs you buy in a store. But they are bigger.

The female does not sit on the eggs. The sun warms the nest. But the female keeps guard. She watches out for bears, skunks, and lizards. These are some of the animals that eat alligator and crocodile eggs.

Sometimes an animal tries to steal some eggs. The mother attacks. Most enemies run away. The mother's sharp teeth and powerful jaws are very scary!

Two or three months pass. The
mother hears chirps from inside the eggs!
The chirps tell her that the eggs are ready
to hatch. She digs the eggs out from the
nest. And she helps the babies break out
of their shells.

Sometimes the babies crawl into the mother's mouth. She gently carries them to the water. Then she opens her mouth. Out they creep.

A female alligator or crocodile seems to be a good mom. She stays close to her babies for a year or more. The mother protects her babies. If an enemy comes close, she hisses or roars. This usually scares the foe away.

Meanwhile, the mother gives her babies piggyback rides. She lets them sit on her head. But she does not feed them. The baby alligator or crocodile must find its own food.

Luckily for them, babies have full sets
of teeth. The teeth are small, but very sharp.
The babies use them to catch small fish,
tadpoles, flies, moths, and beetles.

Baby alligators and crocodiles grow
very quickly. Some gain about a foot a year
for six years. Suppose you grew that fast.
You'd be around seven feet tall!

Chapter Four

Day and Night

Alligators and crocodiles nap on and off all day. Sometimes they sleep in the water. Other times they rest on riverbanks.

When possible, alligators and crocodiles lie in the sun. Their thick skin collects the rays. The sun warms their bodies.

Alligators and crocodiles are cold-blooded animals. Cold-blooded animals must get heat from outside their bodies. Without outside heat, the animals move very slowly.

Alligators and crocodiles live in warm parts of the world where there is a lot of sunshine. When the animals get too hot, they head for the shade. Sometimes they slide back into the water.

When hungry, alligators and crocodiles look for animals to eat. These animals are called prey. Fish, birds, turtles, frogs, and raccoons are favorite prey. Other prey include large animals, such as pigs, deer, dogs, sheep, and cows.

Suppose a crocodile spots a wildebeest (WILL-duh-beest) crossing a river. The crocodile clamps its jaws down on its prey. *SNAP!* The wildebeest cannot escape.

The crocodile grips the wildebeest in its jaws. It drags the wildebeest under the water. The wildebeest drowns. The crocodile pulls the drowned animal onto the land. It uses its sharp teeth to tear the prey apart. Then the crocodile swallows the pieces whole — without chewing!

Alligators and crocodiles have special flaps in their throats. The flaps keep the water out. Other flaps cover their ears and nostrils.

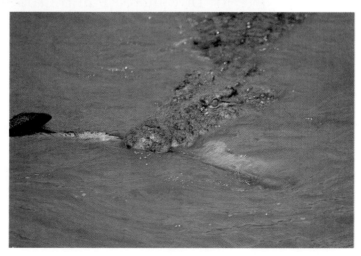

Alligators and crocodiles also have extra eyelids. They're like goggles. They protect the animals' eyes under the water. Yet they also let the animal hunt for food and keep safe.

The teeth of alligators and crocodiles are special. The front ones are very sharp. The animals use them for catching and holding their prey. The teeth in the back are shorter and more blunt. Alligators and crocodiles use them to get the food in place before swallowing.

Alligators and crocodiles lose many teeth. Some get knocked out by their prey. Others become worn and fall out.

Alligators may lose 3,000 teeth in a lifetime! But new teeth are growing in all the time. One tooth falls out. And a new one pops up to take its place.

Alligators and crocodiles look slow and lazy. But don't be fooled. They swim very fast. When chasing prey, an alligator or crocodile can top 20 miles an hour. That's more than twice the speed of the fastest human swimmer!

Believe it or not — alligators and crocodiles have good manners! Let's say a crocodile catches a cow. It tears off a chunk of flesh. And it swims away to enjoy its meal.

Other crocodiles swim over. They rip into the cow. In a while, the first crocodile returns. Only this time it waits its turn to eat again!

Alligators and crocodiles do not eat every day like you do. Once a week is more usual. Some can go without food for as long as two years!

How can alligators and crocodiles go months without eating? The answer is this: They store lots of fat in their bodies. Most of the fat ends up in their tails.

Chemicals in their stomachs break down the food alligators and crocodiles eat. This helps the animals digest what they swallow. As you know, alligators and crocodiles do not chew their food!

Alligators and crocodiles also swallow pebbles. This is not because pebbles taste good. It's because the pebbles weigh them down. This helps the animals float just under the surface of the water. Here they are out of sight and safe from enemies.

Some birds are safe around crocodiles. In fact, the birds even help the crocodiles. Among these birds are white herons and plovers. They often ride on top of the crocodiles. The birds feed on tiny bugs they find there.

A plover sometimes gets food from a crocodile's mouth! The bird hops inside. Here, it acts like a toothpick. The plover pecks out tasty leftovers from between the crocodile's teeth! This gives the plover something to eat. And the crocodile gets a nice, clean mouth.

Chapter Five

All in the Family

Alligators and crocodiles are cousins. They belong to a family of animals called crocodilians (krok-uh-DILL-yuns).

Crocodilians are a very old family. They lived at the time of the dinosaurs. That was over 200 million years ago!

Besides alligators and crocodiles, the crocodilian family includes two other animals. They are **gharials** (GERR-ee-uhlz) and **caimans** (KAY-munz).

Gharials are sometimes called **gavials** (GAY-vee-uhlz). They look more like crocodiles than like alligators. Gharials live only in Asia.

Caimans look more like alligators than like crocodiles. They live in warm parts of North and South America.

Today, there are two kinds of alligators—the American alligator and the Chinese alligator. They live thousands of miles apart. But they look very much alike.

The American alligator has a huge tail. It can be a very powerful weapon. One blow can kill a large enemy. It can even kill a human being.

The Chinese alligator is smaller than the American alligator. This animal is rare and hard to find. There are only about 500 left in the wild.

There are about 12 different kinds of crocodiles. The American crocodile lives mostly in Florida and Central America. It is far less common than the American alligator.

The saltwater crocodile of Asia and Australia is the biggest of all crocodilians. One used to live in Australia's National Zoo. It weighed more than one ton!

The **Nile crocodile** lives in Africa. Some Africans call it "the animal that kills while smiling." Nile crocodiles actually harm more people than lions do!

Crocodilians are amazing creatures. Their ancestors walked with the dinosaurs. Dinosaurs died out millions of years ago. Yet crocodilians are still here. Let's hope they're here to stay!

Index

Africa, 39

alligators, 4–10, 12–15,
17–23, 25–26, 28–32,
34–38

American alligators,
36–38

American crocodiles,
38

Asia, 10, 35–38

Australia, 38

babies, 17–21

birds, 25, 33

caimans, 35–36

Chinese alligators,
36–37

cold-blooded, 23

cows, 25, 31

crocodiles, 7–10,
12–15, 17–23, 25–26,
28–36, 38–39

crocodilians, 34, 38–39

dinosaurs, 34, 39

ears, 26

eggs, 14–15, 17

enemies, 14–15, 18,
32, 37

eyes, 4, 28

fish, 5–6, 20, 25

gharials, 35

hiding, 5, 10, 32

humans, 30, 37, 39

jaws, 6, 15, 26

legs, 7–8, 12

mouths, 9, 18, 33

nests, 12–14, 17

Nile crocodiles, 39

North America, 10, 36–38

nostrils, 5, 26

prey, 25–26, 28–30

rivers, 7, 10, 22, 26

skin, 22

sleeping, 22

snouts, 8–9

South America, 36

sun, 14, 22–23

swallowing, 6, 26, 28, 32

swimming, 5, 7, 10, 30–31

tails, 7–8, 31, 37

teeth, 6, 8–9, 15, 20, 26,
28–29, 33

wildebeests, 26